Reptiles

Komodo Dragons

by Joanne Mattern

Consulting Editor: Gail Saunders-Smith, PhD
Content Consultants: Joe Maierhauser, President/CEO
Terry Phillip, Curator of Reptiles
Reptile Gardens, Rapid City, South Dakota

Capstone
press

Mankato, Minnesota

Pebble Plus is published by Capstone Press,
151 Good Counsel Drive, P.O. Box 669, Mankato, Minnesota 56002.
www.capstonepub.com

Books published by Capstone Press are manufactured with paper
containing at least 10 percent post-consumer waste.

Library of Congress Cataloging-in-Publication Data
Mattern, Joanne, 1963–
    Komodo dragons / by Joanne Mattern.
    p. cm. — (Pebble plus. Reptiles)
    Includes bibliographical references and index.
    Summary: "Simple text and photographs present komodo dragons,
how they look, where they live, and what they do" — Provided by publisher.
    ISBN 978-1-4296-3321-5 (library binding)
    1. Komodo dragon — Juvenile literature. I. Title. II. Series.
QL666.L29M38 2010
597.95'968 — dc22   2008051192

Editorial Credits
Jenny Marks, editor; Matt Bruning, designer; Jo Miller, media researcher

Photo Credits
Getty Images Inc./The Image Bank/Theo Allofs, 9
iStockphoto/Holger Mette, back cover
Minden Pictures/Mark Jones, 11
Nature Picture Library/Michael Pitts, 17
NewsCom, 21
Peter Arnold/WILDLIFE, 5
Shutterstock/capturefoto, 7; Holger Mette, 1; kkaplin, 13, 15; Specta, front cover

Note to Parents and Teachers

The Pebble Plus Reptiles set supports science standards related to life science. This book
describes and illustrates Komodo dragons. The images support early readers in understanding
the text. The repetition of words and phrases helps early readers learn new words. This book
also introduces early readers to subject-specific vocabulary words, which are defined in the
Glossary section. Early readers may need assistance to read some words and to use the Table of
Contents, Glossary, Read More, Internet Sites, and Index sections of the book.

Printed in the United States of America in North Mankato, Minnesota.
112010
006003R

Table of Contents

A Huge Lizard

Komodo dragons are the largest lizards in the world. They grow up to 10 feet (3 meters) long.

Komodo dragons have
strong legs and long tails.
Males weigh up to
300 pounds (136 kilograms).
Females are smaller.

A Komodo's Home

Komodo dragons live in Indonesia.

Indonesia is a country

made up of hot, dry islands.

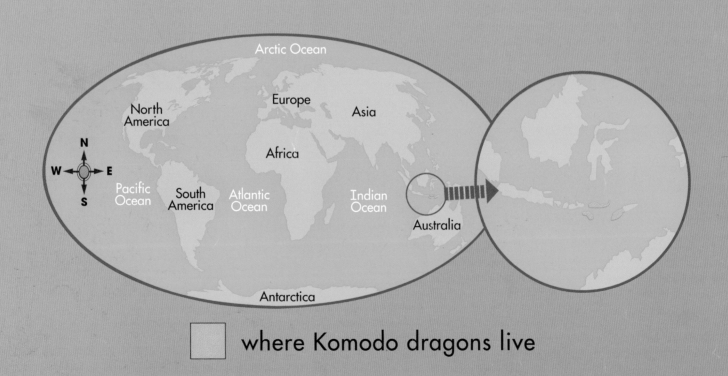

where Komodo dragons live

Komodo dragons crawl

on the ground.

They hide under trees.

These lizards are also

good swimmers.

A Dangerous Animal

Komodo dragons are predators.

They eat goats, deer, and pigs.

Their sharp teeth and claws

tear apart prey.

A Komodo dragon's mouth
is full of germs.
One bite can kill its prey.
Then the Komodo
eats the dead animal.

A Komodo's Life

Komodo dragons

hatch from eggs.

Females lay 20 to 40 eggs

in the sand.

The Komodo's eggs hatch
about eight months later.
After hatching, Komodos
take care of themselves.
They live for 20 to 40 years.

Komodo Dragon Life Cycle

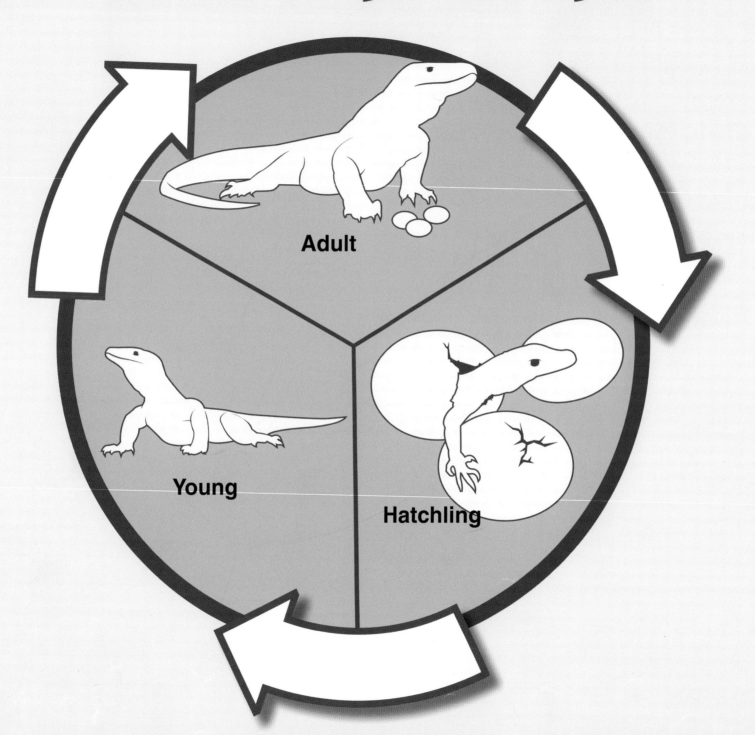

Adult

Young

Hatchling

Saving Komodos

Only 5,000 Komodos

live in the wild.

They are endangered.

People are trying to save

these big lizards.

Glossary

endangered — in danger of dying out

germ — a very small living organism that can cause sickness

hatch — to break out of an egg

lizard — a reptile with a scaly body and a long tail

predator — an animal that hunts other animals for food

prey — an animal hunted by another animal for food

Read More

Lunis, Natalie. *Komodo Dragon: The World's Biggest Lizard*. SuperSized! New York: Bearport Pub., 2007.

Maynard, Thane. *Komodo Dragons*. New Naturebooks. Chanhassen, Minn.: Child's World, 2007.

O'Donnell, Kerri. *Komodo Dragons*. Ugly Animals. New York: PowerKids Press, 2007.

Internet Sites

FactHound offers a safe, fun way to find Internet sites related to this book. All of the sites on FactHound have been researched by our staff.

Here's all you do:

Visit *www.facthound.com*

FactHound will fetch the best sites for you!

Index

Word Count: 161
Grade: 1
Early-Intervention Level: 20